Fighting Sexual Temptation

An Attack of the Heart

by

Anthony J. Carter

east point books
POINTING PEOPLE TO CHRIST

PO Box 90818 • East Point GA • 30364

Fighting Sexual Temptation
© 2010 by Anthony J. Carter

Published by East Point Books
A ministry of East Point Church
PO Box 90818
East Point, GA 30364

All rights reserved.

Unless otherwise noted all Scripture quotations are from *The Holy Bible, English Standard Version*, copyright © 2001 by Crossway Bibles, a publishing ministry of Good News Publishers. Used by permission.

Printed in the United States of America

"Satan gives Adam an apple (fruit), and takes away Paradise. Therefore in all temptations let us consider not what he offers, but what we shall lose."

- Richard Sibbes

An Attack of the Heart

Sex sells. This is a truth of which those who market products are acutely aware. Whether it is beer or protein juice, deodorant or shampoo, a scantily clothed young lady or seductress appealing to our baser instincts seems to be the most popular method of pitching products today. You can't avoid it. Television commercials are filled with it, billboards abound, and even radio ads entice the imagination with flirtatious voices and innuendos. Sexually explicit messages sent through text messaging are so popular in some circles that it has a name, "sexting." With such an incessant appeal to sexuality in our culture, one is left to wonder how to survive the minefield that is sexual temptation. Sex is not just in the city. It is in the country, the prairie, the desert, on the oceanfront, and everywhere in between.

A friend once asked me how I keep myself from sexual temptation. My response to him was that I don't. Initially he was taken back by my response and thought I was going to lay on him some unforgivable tale of marital infidelity. I comforted him by informing him that while I am not able to keep myself from temptation, I am (by God's grace and faithfulness) endeavoring to keep myself from sexual sin. It is not easy. Temptation is all around us. To take one's self away from temptation is to take one's self out of the world. It was Martin Luther, the 16th century German monk, who said, "I can't keep the birds from flying over my head, but I can keep them from nesting in my hair." The fight against temptation and sin is not a fight to keep temptation from ever flying over your head; it is more a fight to keep sin from making a home in your heart. This is particularly true with sexual sin. The issue is the heart. And our Lord says as much in Matthew 7:27-30:

> **"You have heard that it was said, 'You shall not commit adultery.' But I say to you that everyone who looks at a woman with lustful intent has already committed adultery with her in his heart. If your right eye causes you to sin, tear it out and throw it away. For it is better that you lose one of your members than that your whole body be thrown into hell. And if your right hand causes you to sin, cut it off and throw it away. For it is better that you lose one of your members than that your whole body go into hell.**

When addressing the issue of sexual temptation, the core of Jesus' teaching was addressed to the heart of men and women. Sexual sin, like all sin, is conceived in the heart. Therefore it is in the heart that the battle against sexual sin is either won or lost. It is the discontented heart that fuels the lust of the flesh. Only by informing our hearts and minds with the words of our Lord against sinful lust will we be empowered to navigate the sexual temptations around us. To this end, this book looks briefly at the above passage and sees that Jesus gives us a *command against lust;* tells us how to *curb our lust;* and offers the path to *contentment in place of lust.*

Putting Jesus' Words in Context

Here Jesus takes up the proper and God-honoring understanding of the 7th commandment. He says to those gathered with him, "You have heard it said, 'You shall not commit adultery.'" Of course, when Jesus originally spoke these words in the Sermon on the Mount, those listening had heard this command before. His audience was filled with Jewish people who would have been particularly familiar with His words. No doubt they would have heard the command not to comment adultery countless times. It comes straight from the law of God through His servant Moses in Exodus 20:14 and Deuteronomy 5:18. It is the seventh of the Ten Commandments. Every man or woman and every boy or girl of age would have known what the 7th Commandment said. But not only would they have known what it said, they also would have known what the punishment for violating that command would have been. In Leviticus 20 and Deuteronomy 22 we are told that those who committed such an act would have been put to death.

Death for adultery. It seems a bit harsh in our times because we have become so accustomed to marital infidelity. We have learned to live in a world and in families that are ravaged by it. And yet God never wants his people to get used to any sin, and especially not adultery. Adultery is an awful sin for several reasons.

It is first and foremost a sin against God. Adultery says to God that God is not enough. It says, "I must have more than he gives me. I must have more than he can offer." It says that God's wisdom and timing are erroneous and misplaced. It says that I know better than God does – I know best. It is the manifestation of a heart that is not satisfied with God and His direction of our lives. Thus, it impugns God's character and defames his name. No wonder David prayed and confessed after he had sinned with Bathsheba: *"Against you, and you only, have I sinned and done what is evil in your sight"* (Ps. 51:3).

It is also a sin against the most sacred trust. It violates the most sacred bond and covenant one person can make with another. To pledge oneself in marriage to another is the highest and most God-like expression of covenant love we human beings can experience on earth. So lofty and holy is this expression that God has chosen it to demonstrate the love that he has for his people. The divine marriage covenant prefigured in God and his relationship with the nation of Israel (Isa. 54:5), today is fulfilled in Christ and his relationship with the Church (Eph. 5:22-32).

It is also a sin against community. The sanctity and prosperity of a community is based upon the familial structure of that community. When a community is in the throes of collapse and ruin, you can almost certainly attribute the destruction in large measure to the destruction of family and marital covenant bonds. For if a man or a woman is willing to violate the covenant of marriage, should he or she be expected or counted on to keep his or her covenant with others in the community? If his spouse cannot trust him, who can?

God knew the critical roles marriages and covenant keeping need to play in a community, particularly in a community of faith. So the command against adultery is understandable. And while we would not advocate a death sentence for adulterers, we should understand why the death penalty would have been invoked in a community and time where people relied so heavily upon the truth and justice of that community for survival.

Furthermore, Jesus does not simply remind the people of what they already knew, but he (as he would frequently do) takes it to another level. He not only reminds them of what the law said, but he also tells them what the Law means.

This is always the crux of the issue. We frequently do not mind people telling us what the Bible *says*. Our issue comes when we are brought face to face with what it *means*. We want the meaning to be left up to us. But Jesus does not give his disciples this luxury, nor does he give it to us today. And thus, Jesus says to his listeners, "I know you have heard the commandment, but do you understand that even to look upon a woman with lustful intentions in your heart is to violate the law of God."

A Commandment Against Lust

When Jesus here invokes the violation of the law in the heart before the violating of the law with the hands, he is not introducing anything knew, but is simply rightly interpreting the law of God. He is reminding them that this is what the law has always meant. The Pharisees and the teachers of the law (and like most of us today) perceived that the law was written so that people would be accountable to other people. While it does serve this purpose, Jesus here reminds us that the primary intent of the law is to cause us to understand our accountability before God. We read in 1Sam. 16:7: *For the Lord sees not as man sees, man looks on the outward appearance, but the Lord looks on the heart.*

The heart is the seat of our motivations. It is here that we really live before God and it is the place where we are measured for our actions. It is the heart of men and women that God must change if we are ever going to do anything that pleases Him. Even outward worship that appears to be full of excitement and joy may be of no profit or value to God because the hearts of those excited and joyful are not after him. Jesus says in Matt. 15:8: *"This people honor me with their lips, but their hearts are from me."*

We all know that it is possible to have someone's lip service but not their heart service. In the Sermon on the Mount Jesus says that a man or a woman who gives lip service to their spouse but not heart service is an adulterer. Here Jesus again illustrates what it means for our righteousness to exceed the righteousness of the Pharisees (Matt. 5:20). The Pharisees knew the command not to commit adultery and sought to keep it. Jesus says that those who are of His kingdom understand that they are not only to refrain from the act of adultery, but the grace and mercy of God to them causes them to stifle even the thought of such an act. The kingdom way is not just the way of the flesh, but it is the way of the heart.

A man or woman may be doing outwardly what they need to do, but everyday and in numerous ways, their hearts wander, and they are in affect committing adultery. Adultery, like all sins, originates in the heart. And while we do not work out everything that is in our heart (thank God), God still holds us accountable not only for the sin we do, but even for the sin we wish to do if only we had opportunity. God sees the heart of men and women and declares: *"For out of the heart come evil thoughts, murder, adultery, sexual immorality, theft, false witness, and slander"* (Matt. 15:19).

The heart is the place of our meditation and contemplation. It is where our desires lie. It is where our lusts originate. Jesus here reminds us that we have sinned gravely not when we have looked at that woman or man, but when we have looked and lusted after them. And let us not be mistaken. The command is not just for men toward women or even women toward men. It is also a command against men toward men and women toward women. All of these find God's condemnation outside of the biblical bounds of marriage between one man and one woman.

What then is lust? Lust is an inordinate, excessive, and (biblically speaking) sinful coveting of something or someone. We know of people who lust for money, for power, for fame and fortune, prestige and pleasure. And we have seen how these lustful desires lead to self destruction. Jesus reminds us that if we are not diligent in dealing with them at their root, the lust of sexual desires will lead to destruction as well. In other words, the only cure for the sinful fruit of lust is to chop that tree at its roots and those roots lay in the heart and that to which we expose our hearts.

An Attack of the Heart

Curbing Our Lust

Those hearing Jesus would have thought his words more radical than we do today. Many of the men and women standing there listening to Jesus would have thought to themselves that they had never violated the 7th commandment? They would have said with confidence that they had never cheated on their spouse or caused a married person to cheat on theirs. They would have thought themselves safe and secure in their righteousness - that is until Jesus *interprets* the 7th commandment and indicts nearly every man and woman under the sound of his voice.

Radical were his words and yet, even more radical was his solution. The way to curb lust in our hearts, according to Jesus, is the cutting off or throwing down of those things by which the temptation to lust comes, namely your eyes (what you see) and your hands (what you do).

Blinding our Eyes

Though some have taken Jesus literally, and have unfortunately mutilated themselves in an attempt to destroy the temptation to sin, Jesus is not here saying that you should literally take your eye out of your head and walk around blind. What he is saying however is that we must exist as if that which desires to tempt us visually does not exist. Jesus says elsewhere, *"The eye is the lamp of the body. So, if your eye is healthy, your whole body will be full of light" (Matt. 6:22).*

As such we must be diligent in what we find gaining the attention of our eyes. Admittedly this is not easy in our sex-crazed society. Everywhere you turn - whether sitting at home in front of the television or at work in front of the computer, whether watching a movie at a theater or just walking in the park - your eyes are nearly blinded by sexually explicit connotations and innuendo. Several points could be made in this regard.

Firstly, too often the movies we regard as "girl flicks" are nothing more than propaganda for illicit and extra-marital affairs. So-called "date movies" often serve as visual foreplay encouraging sexual playfulness and pre-marital encounters.

Secondly, according to a recent study by the Kaiser Family Foundation, sexual content on TV has soared since 1998. The sampling was taken from more than 1,000 hours of television programming outside of newscasts, sports events, and children shows. All sexual content was measured, including talk about sex and sexual behavior. The study was taken from a variety of networks including ABC, CBS, NBC, FOX, WB, PBS, TNT, USA, HBO, and Lifetime. The following was discovered:

1. In 1998 56% of all shows contained sexual content
2. In 2002 64% of all shows contained sexual content
3. In 2005 70% of all shows contained sexual content
4. During prime-time hours the rate shot up to 77% with an average of nearly 7 sex scenes per hour.[1]

What is the result of this flippant, casual, and perverted view of sex in our society? We see the increase of the abuse and misuse of women and children. We have the rise and perpetuation of shame and guilt. We witness more frequently the disintegration of marriage and fidelity. And we see the continuing desecration of vows and promises.

A continued diet of infidelity and innuendo will inevitably desensitize us to the awful reality of sexual sin. We must acknowledge that this diet comes primarily through our eye gate. The question we must be willing to ask is, "What are we watching?" Job, in recognizing the potential of temptation and sin through the faculty of our eyes, made this remark: *"I made a covenant with my eyes not to look lustfully at a girl"* (Job 31:1 NIV).

Lead not into Temptation

I do believe at this point, if we are going to be faithful to this sensitive and penetrating subject, then we must mention the point of leading others into temptation. I am speaking mainly here concerning the call for women in

---

[1] http://www.kff.org/entmedia/entmedia110905nr.cfm

particular, but all of us in general, to dress in a manner that reflects our desire not to tempt others to sin.

Jesus prayed in the model prayer, "Lead us not into temptation" (Matt. 6:13). Obviously, he was teaching us how we are to pray to God the Father. And yet, is that not also my request to you and your request to me? I pray that none of you would lead me into temptation and that I in like manner would not lead you into temptation. Jesus also reminds us in Matt. 18:7: *"Woe to the world for temptations to sin! For it is necessary that temptations come, but woe to the one by whom the temptation comes."*

In other words, Jesus reminds us that the world is fraught with temptation. If we are going to live without any temptations, then we would have to totally and absolutely remove ourselves from the world. Since this is neither possible nor advisable (1Cor. 5:10), we must live with the tension of these temptations and stumbling blocks remaining all around us. And while this is necessary in the world, why do we so often find the same temptations in the church?

I understand that modest dress is not a popular idea today. This is particularly true in light of the hotter climates of the southern states where I make my home. However, the Bible says not only should we not tempt each other to sin, but women should come to church in modest, respectful, and virtuous clothing (1 Tim. 2:9). Unfortunately, too often this is not the case.

Ladies, in case you were not aware of it, every man I know, young and old, knows the struggle of fighting temptation and lust. It is not an easy battle. Some, by God's grace, have gained some control over it and are mercifully living in freedom. However, many have not and are in a constant battle with their minds and heart for control of their thoughts. What are you doing to help or hinder them? Are you aware that the biggest stumbling block comes from the clothes that women too often choose to wear?

We unavoidably behold blouses that are cut too low, skirts that are too high, and midriffs that are constantly on display. Then there are tattoos often purposely placed in seductive places for the purpose of grabbing attention and enticing lustful thoughts. Women, you may not think much of such things, but I can tell you for sure that the men around you notice and struggle to maintain their thought life even at church.

The world is full of scantily dress women, who cause us to do a double take. But the church of Jesus Christ should not be such a place. We must discern the difference between being attractive and seductive. If you are not sure, then ask the men in your life. If they are honest they will tell you when your dress is too revealing or not.[2]

Ladies, I do understand the difficulty here. My wife frequently informs me how difficult it is to find nice, modest clothing today for her and our daughters. The fashion world is not interested in godly standards. David Brooks, journalist and social commentator, has rightly said:

> *The average square yardage of boys' fashion grows and grows while the square inches in the girls' outfits shrink and shrink, so that while the boys look like tent-wearing skateboarders, the girls look like preppy prostitutes.*[3]

When it comes to fashion, clearly the world is not a friend to the church. I understand that it is not easy finding fashionable clothes today. I am not suggesting that Christians dress totally out of date and embrace the fashions of Little House on the Prairie. However, I am confident that with a little effort we can dress in a way that represents biblical attractiveness and encourages the faith of others as well. Yes, it will take some effort today but are not your brothers worth the extra effort? Is not the glory

---

[2] Another helpful resource to consider when accessing modesty in dress is the *Modesty Heart Check*. You can find a copy of it online at http://girltalk.blogs.com/girltalk/files/modesty_heart_check3.pdf

[3] Quoted in *Sermon on the Mount: The Character of a Disciple*, Daniel M. Doriani (Philipsburg, NJ: P&R Publishing, 2006), p. 64

Jesus Christ our Lord and Savior and the sake of the gospel worth the effort as well?

When our children were younger they yearly attended Cedine Bible Camp in Spring City, TN. Every year before they would leave we received in our home the dress code for camp. Here is what Cedine Camp required:

Please dress modestly at all times…

<u>Females</u>:
1. *Pants, skirts and shorts should not be tight fitting or revealing. Shorts must be at or past fingertips when arms are at sides.*
2. *No spaghetti straps, low cleavage tops, halter tops, or men muscle shirts.*
3. *Tops must be long enough to cover waist when arms are extended above the head, when bending over or sitting.*
4. *One piece swim suits only.*

<u>Males</u>:
1. *Shirts must be worn at all times in the area. No muscle shirts.*
2. *Pants/Shorts must be comfortable, but not dropping or overly sagging.*

Now, I am not here seeking to implement a dress code at any church. Nor am I pushing for any sort of dress police standing at the door. Inevitably such behavior will only produce self-righteousness and judgment, which are potentially more destructive to the spirit than spaghetti straps. However, I find it interesting that we would have standards for camp, but no standards or loose standards for church. We all know the reason why the camp would have such standards. Are we so naïve as to believe that the church is not a place of similar temptations?

Recently I read an article on modesty by Nancy Leigh DeMoss. In the article she quoted Richard Baxter, a 17th century pastor, concerning the need for modesty among women in his day. Baxter wrote:

> *And though it be their sin and vanity that is the cause, it is nevertheless your sin to be the unnecessary occasion…You must not lay a stumbling-block in their way, nor blow up the fire of their lust…You must walk among sinful persons, as you would do with a candle among straw or gunpowder; or else you may see the flame which you did not foresee, when it is too late to quench it.*[4]

Our society is far more relaxed in its standards of modesty than that of Baxter. If the issue was a concern in his day, how much more is it in ours?

Women, ultimately the sin lies in the heart of men. As men, we must learn to discipline our bodies and keep them under control (1 Cor. 9:27). Nevertheless, let's make sure that you are helping your brothers on this quest for victory and not hindering them. Temptations are sure to come, but woe to those by whom the temptation comes!

---

[4] Quoted in **Revive our Hearts** Summer 2007 Newsletter, Nancy Leigh DeMoss, *"Does God Really Care What I Wear?"*

Contentment in Place of Lust

Jesus says that the way to curb lust is the cutting off of those things that invite temptation to us. Whether it is our hand and/or eye, Jesus says that it is better for us to cut these things (these valuable and useful things) off and save our souls than to keep these things and enter into hell because of our reluctance to deal with sin.

Yet, when we think about the gravity of our Lord's words, and if we could put ourselves in the position of those who first heard Jesus speaking, we might ask the question, "Why would anyone cut off a member of their own body?" Again, obviously Jesus is not saying to literally cut out an eye or to literally make oneself lame. Nevertheless, if the Kingdom of God and heaven itself are my goals, then I will be determined to gain entry by any means necessary. I may appear to look foolish to the world; I may appear to be out of step with the times, but I must be convinced that the present world is not worthy of comparison to the world to come.

My hands and my eyes are means of bringing to me things that promise satisfaction, pleasure, and contentment. For the faithful the question is where or in whom do we find our satisfaction, pleasure, and contentment. The bottom line is whether or not I am contented with Christ. Is Jesus enough for me? Am I willing to do whatever I must in order to have more of Christ? Am I willing to do as the Bible said Moses did, who chose *"rather to be mistreated with the people of God than to enjoy the fleeting pleasures of sin"* (Heb. 11:25)? Are we heeding the command of Scripture to have our minds and affections set upon those things that are above and not on those things which are on earth (Col. 3:2)?

Are we obeying the command to set our thoughts on whatever things are true, honorable, just, pure, lovely, commendable, excellent, and praise worthy (Phil 4:8)? Am I willing to set aside the sin in my life that I too frequently enjoy? Am I killing sin or is sin killing me? Am I beating my flesh into subjection, or is my flesh beating me into sin? Brothers and Sisters, I know killing sin is not easy. Even in the process of writing this material I am reminded of how easily my eyes and my heart can wander. I am again and again reminded of Paul's words in Rom. 7:18-19:

> *For I know that nothing good dwells in me, that is, in my flesh. For I have the desire to do what is right, but not the ability to carry it out. For I do not do the good I want, but the evil I do not want is what I keep on doing.*

He goes on to ask the all-important question,
> *"O wretched man that I am, who shall deliver me from this body of death?"* (Rom. 7:24).

Brothers and Sisters, we must flee from sexual immorality and flee all forms of temptation whether it is in our flesh or in our minds (1Cor. 6:8; 10:14). But in fleeing

An Attack of the Heart

we must not just run for the sake of running; we must run to the right place. And where is that? We must run to Calvary. We must run to the cross. Consequently, the Apostle Paul answers his question of deliverance by thanking God for Jesus Christ our Lord (Rom. 7:25).

When we look to the Cross of Christ we see there a Savior who is able to save and satisfy. We see a Savior who was like us, in every way tempted and yet without sin (Heb. 4:15). There we see a Savior whose body was broken and whose blood was shed so that our sins no longer have rule or sway in our lives. We see a Savior who by his sacrifice broke the power of sin and Satan in our lives. There we see a Savior who in place of the temporary and fleeting satisfaction of unlawful sex, offers himself as a superior, complete, and eternal satisfaction to his people.

Sexual temptation is strong and in our times often ubiquitous. Those who claim never to have been exposed or even fallen prey to it are either lying or have lived with their head in the sand. None of us are immune to it, and if we are honest, no one can say they have been kept pure from it. Nevertheless, we never need live as slaves to it or to find ourselves perpetrators of it. We have Christ!

Therefore, when your mind begins to think upon illicit things, when you heart begins to wander after that which does not belong to you, and when Satan then comes and seeks to tempt you finally to fall because you have sinned already, what shall you do? Give in fully to the temptation? God forbid!

Remember the words of the song writer:

When Satan tempts me to despair
And tells me of the guilt within;
Upward I look and see him there
Who made an end to all my sin.

If you are in Christ, He has made an end to all your sin. He has nailed your sins to the cross and has cancelled the debt and guilt associated with it. You are no longer held captive to this sin and have been given direction in the Bible and empowerment by the Spirit to live in victory over it. It was Augustine who prayed, "God command what you will. And grant what you command." Christ commands us to keep our hearts from lust. Then he graciously grants us all we need to fulfill his commands. Apostle Paul's declaration that he *"disciplined* (literally "pummeled") *his body to keep it under subjection,"* was built upon the all-important understanding and conviction:

"I have been crucified with Christ. It is no longer I who live, but Christ who lives in me. And the life I now live in the flesh, I live by faith in the Son of God, who loved me and gave himself for me" (Gal. 2:20).

Therefore, let us live for Him who is able to save and satisfy us, Him who can keep us from stumbling and present us faultless before the presence of God in glory with joy (Jude 1:24). Now and forever. Amen.

An Attack of the Heart

ABOUT THE AUTHOR

Anthony J. Carter is the lead pastor of East Point Church in East Point, GA. He is the author and/or editor of several books including *On Being Black and Reformed* and *Glory Road: The Journeys of 10 African-Americans into Reformed Christianity*. Besides his duties as a pastor, he is the husband of Adriane and the father of Anthony Jr., Rachel, Sarah, Siera, and Ana. They live in East Point, GA where he enjoys studying, golf, and chillin' with the family.

For more information on East Point Church or to order more copies of this book, visit online at www.epointchurch.org.

Or write:

East Point Church
PO Box 90818
East Point, GA 30364

An Attack of the Heart

Made in the USA
Charleston, SC
01 May 2011